Paper
Pop-Ups

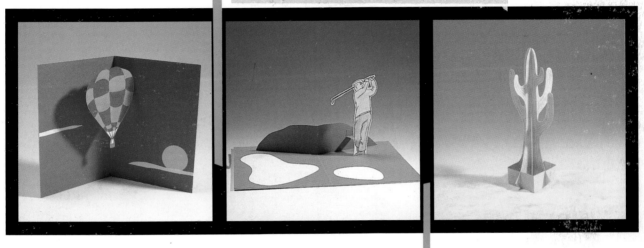

First published in the United States of America by:
Quarry Books, an imprint of
Rockport Publishers, Inc.
146 Granite Street
Rockport, Massachusetts 01966-1299
Telephone: (508) 546-9590
Fax: (508) 546-7141

Distributed to the book trade and art trade in the United States by:
North Light, an imprint of
F&W Publications
1507 Dana Avenue
Cinncinnati, Ohio 45207
Telephone: (513) 531-2222

ISBN 1-56496-170-2

2 4 6 8 10 9 7 5 3 1

Designer
Kristen Webster
Blue Sky Limited

Photography
Paul Forrester

Manufactured in Hong Kong by Excel Printing

Paper Pop-Ups

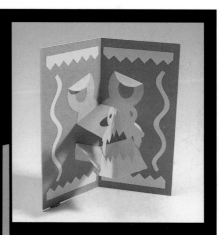

Paul Jackson

QUARRY BOOKS
Rockport, Massachusetts

Contents

Introduction

W hat is a pop-up? The best answer is that pop-ups are absolutely the finest greeting cards you can send or receive! They are ingenious and fun, a wonderful mixture of magic and geometry that never fails to bring a smile when an unfamiliar design is opened for the first time. A pop-up is more than just a card; it is an object to be displayed and admired long after other cards have been put away.

The technical definition of just what is and is not a pop-up differs among designers. For me, it is a three-dimensional structure that automatically erects itself from within when unfolded. Some designers include two-dimensional effects such as rotating disks, dissolving scenes, or pull-tab movements in this definition, but for me, they lack the magic of a true pop-up and are not included in this book.

The construction of pop-up books and greeting cards began in London during the 1850s, but the geometric principles behind them go much farther back. Selferecting structures have been used for centuries by people as diverse as stage illusionists, cabinet makers, and origami designers, and since the beginning of time by Mother Nature—just watch how a flower opens. In recent years, pop-up books have become ever-more spectacular as designers try to outdo their rivals to achieve greater sales. Some of the results are truly amazing!

And yet, pop-up techniques are essentially simple. This book introduces six of the most versatile techniques with a number of basic—but interesting—projects. Some are explained in step-by-step detail with photographs, while the *Gallery* spreads show photographs or drawings of completed projects. With over forty-five projects in the book, everyone can find something to make. You are also encouraged to change or adapt the projects to your own specifications, rather than just copy the instructions.

But before starting a pop-up, I recommend you read *How to Use This Book*, the *Glossary & Key*, and the *Basics* section. They give invaluable advice to guide you smoothly through the design, decoration, and construction of the pop-up. Most importantly, remember that pop-ups must be made with precision, and that precision comes from thinking clearly, working patiently, and taking pride in what you make. Adopt this positive approach, and your diligence will be hugely rewarded!

I have had great fun designing the pop-ups in this book and truly hope that you will have as good a time making them.

–Paul Jackson

How to Use This Book

Each pop-up project begins with a list of materials and pictures of the finished pop-up. The paper elements at the back of the book are marked with folding lines for your first attempts, and the templates can be traced to make an endless supply of pop-up patterns. To get the best possible results, the three most important things to keep in mind are: cut slowly and carefully, fold precisely, and get to know the Key. The *Glossary & Key* explains the fold lines that appear on each paper element and template at the end of this book. If you are already familiar with this system of folding notation, you will feel right at home; otherwise, spend a few moments learning to recognize these symbols and to understand the terminology.

Begin by cutting out all paper elements for the desired project from the supply sheets provided at the back of the book. You may want to photocopy both the paper elements and the templates, so that you will have extras for practice or in case of a mistake. Study the step-by-step photos carefully, to visually check your work. It is often helpful to look ahead at the next photo to see the results of a fold in advance. Take time to perform the folds neatly and accurately. Some paper elements and templates have been labeled to show where to use an adhesive (either a spray adhesive or glue) to secure important pieces of your pop-up design. The *Gallery* at the end of each section offers variations on each pop-up style, for added inspiration.

Blue tracing templates are included for each project, so that you can make additional pop-ups by tracing the template shapes onto the paper of your choice. Use a photocopier to enlarge the templates to any size you want.

ARTWORK

———— GLUE HERE

Glossary & Key

Because the photos can show only a segment of a project's folding procedure, it is helpful to know whether the paper is being folded in front or from behind. The origami system of valley-folds and mountain-folds uses two kinds of broken lines (see key diagrams) to show when to fold toward the project's surface (valley-fold) and when to fold behind the surface (mountain-fold).

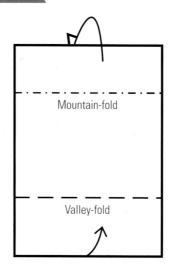

Mountain-fold

Valley-fold

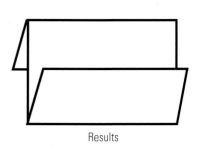

Results

Valley-fold—Relative to the displayed view of the paper being folded, a valley-fold is always folded in front of the project's surface. If you were to unfold a valley-fold you would see a valley-crease, which dents into the paper's surface, forming a valley.

Standard Symbols

Valley-fold — — — — —

Mountain-fold ▬ · ▬ · ▬ · ▬ · ▬

Mountain-fold—Relative to the displayed view of the paper being folded, a mountain-fold is always folded behind the project's surface. If you were to unfold a mountain-fold you would see a mountain-crease, which rises up from the paper's surface, forming a mountain ridge.

Gutter crease—This is a valley-fold in the backing sheet that supports the pop-up.

Backing sheet—The mat board that makes the stiff backing for the pop-up.

Covering layer—The paper that covers the mat board.

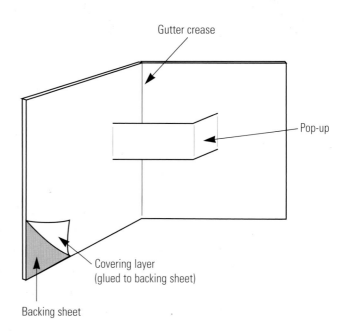

Gutter crease

Pop-up

Covering layer
(glued to backing sheet)

Backing sheet

Basics

Papers and Cardboards

The range of papers and cardboards available to you depends on two factors: where you live, and how much time and energy you are prepared to invest. Cities, larger towns, and shopping centers have art, craft, and office supply stores, which usually stock a wide range of quality papers and cardboards in attractive colors. The choice will be more limited at smaller stores away from major centers, but this selection will be wholly adequate for most pop-up projects. In truth, being able to find only a very limited range of basic white paper and cardboard is sufficient, particularly if you are prepared to decorate it to add color and texture (see *Decorating Paper Ideas*).

With a little more time and effort, a wider range of papers and cardboards can be obtained from other sources. Many wholesale paper suppliers sell (or even give away!) sample pads of papers and cardboards from their range, which are extremely useful if you are reluctant to buy a large sheet from a store, only to use a small piece of it. Small printers frequently have scraps or larger sheets of paper that they will sell to you at a very low cost.

If you are unable to purchase papers and cardboards, consider recycling. Use old cereal boxes, record album covers, chocolate boxes, wrapping paper, junk mail, magazine pages, scrap photocopies, old computer printouts, typing paper, and so on. The list is endless. These seemingly unlikely materials are a wonderful, virtually free source of colorful images and textures to make inspiring pop-ups.

An important consideration when selecting a paper or cardboard is its weight. The backing sheet (see *How to Make a Backing Sheet*) needs to be stiff; otherwise it will not open completely flat. The pop-up that collapses inside it when the backing sheet is closed shut needs to be made from paper or cardboard strong enough to support itself without flopping when the design is opened, but not so thick that it prevents the backing sheet from closing around it. That said, precise weights are unimportant. All that needs to be remembered is that the medium weight paper, thick paper, or thin cardboard used to make the pop-up must be thinner than the cardboard used to make the backing sheet.

Never store paper or cardboard in a roll. The longer it is kept rolled up, the more difficult it will be to flatten. Instead, lay it flat in a safe place under a bed, between sheets of thick cardboard, in an artist's portfolio, or in a large drawer. Larger sheets can be cut into more manageable sizes for easy storage.

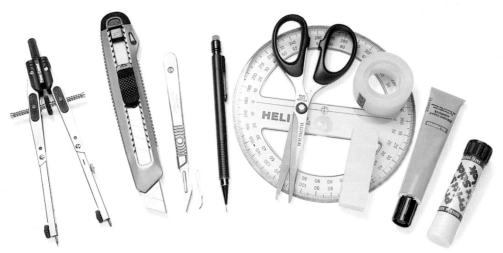

Equipment

In the arts and crafts field, a degree of snobbishness often exists among experienced practitioners regarding the best equipment to use. When making pop-ups, however, most of the equipment can be obtained inexpensively from a local stationery store. There is no mythology about who manufactures the sharpest utility knife or the most efficient erasers. The rule is simple: Buy the best that you can afford. Even the cheapest equipment will suffice, though you will enjoy using the equipment more if it is of better quality.

The one specialty item recommended is the selfhealing cutting mat. These magical mats heal any cut made by a blade, so that the surface never becomes rutted, as wood or thick cardboard would. For the craftsperson who works with a blade, such mats are indispensable; treated well, they will last for many years. Use an adhesive (either a spray adhesive or glue) to attach a cover to a backing sheet, or to secure important pieces, such as tabs, of your pop-up design. Apply them carefully and in small amounts, and use a damp cloth to clean up any excess glue.

The only other item of equipment worth mentioning separately is the cutting blade. It is inadvisable to purchase the cheapest types of retractable, snap-off blade knives. They are not very sturdy and not totally safe when cutting heavier cardboards. If you wish to purchase such a knife, buy a sturdy model that securely locks the retractable blade into cutting position. A better buy is an X-Acto-type knife with blades that can be replaced. The blades usually are sharper and make more precise cuts.

Decorating Paper Ideas

The first and most important point to make about decorating papers and cardboards for pop-ups is that they need not be decorated at all! Quality materials left plain will look stunning, because the different facets of the pop-ups will create subtle and beautiful patterns of light and shade across the structure. By contrast, overly decorated surfaces flatten the pop-up, because the two-dimensional patterns dominate the three-dimensional form. Thus, a modestly decorated surface will look more 3-D than an overly decorated one. The principle then, is to use restraint.

If you are going to decorate, try to use nonwater-based materials. Water crinkles paper and cardboard, so avoid gouache or watercolor paints, which also frequently crack along the line of a crease to leave an unsightly scar.

It is better to use gentler materials, such as marker pens, felt-tipped pens, colored pencils, pastels, or chalks. Pastels or chalks will need a coat of artist's fixative spray if they are not to smudge when the pop-up closes (a less expensive alternative is unscented hairspray—it does the job just as well!).

Or try using other decorating materials. Consider photographs, photocopies, fabric, ribbon, glitter, sequins, flower petals, lipstick, metallic foil, acetate— anything flat! These materials may not be practical to use on commercially mass-produced greeting cards, but there is no reason why they cannot be used on handmade cards.

When to Make a Pop-Up

This may seem curious in a basics section, but the many occasions when one could make a pop-up card are not immediately apparent. We all like to receive greeting cards on important occasions or after an event of personal significance, so someone, somewhere, would love to receive a pop-up from you right now! Here is a list of obvious and not-so-obvious occasions. You can probably think of others.

Birthday	*Wedding*	*Engagement*	*Baptism*	*New Year*
Halloween	*Graduation*	*Get Well*	*Sorry*	*Valentine's Day*
Promotion	*New job*	*Birth of child*	*Retirement*	*Moving away*
Congratulations	*Mother's Day*	*Father's Day*	*Anniversary*	*Yom Kippur*
Rosh Hashanah	*Hanukkah*	*Christmas*	*Easter*	*Thanksgiving*

Embossed paper

Personalizing a Pop-Up

The pop-up projects photographed and drawn in the book all have one vital element missing from each design: a written message or personal greeting. When you make your own pop-up cards, don't forget to include it as part of the design. In fact, it is important to personalize a handmade card as much as possible so that it has personal meaning for the recipient. The pop-ups in the book look, by necessity, a little neutral, so please add, subtract, or change anything and everything so that the card you make is unique to you. In a way, the less like a store-bought, mass-produced, commercial card a pop-up card looks, the more it will be appreciated by the person who receives it, even if it looks a little amateurish. Remember, it is the thought that counts, not the slick-ness of your technique.

Make a Rough, Then Make It Right

Pop-ups are geometric structures that must be designed and assembled with precision. Because of this, you are strongly advised to make a *rough*, or a trial version, before attempting to make a finished design. Not only will the rough teach you a method for designing and assembling the pop-up, but it will also make you aware of how you can successfully deviate from the instructions in the book to make something more personal to you than what is shown.

You may be tempted to skip the rough stage and make a finished pop-up from scratch, but this will probably end in frustration, wasting both time and materials. Use scrap materials to construct the rough, or better still, use the same papers and cardboards as the finished design will be made from so that you can check that all is well with your choice. Making a rough will also give you the opportunity to test any decorative ideas that you may have: Will that green colored pencil stand out on the orange paper? Is the decorative border too dominant? What kind of calligraphic flourish looks best on the backing sheet?

All the necessary tests can be done at this stage: cutting out the pop-up, taping on new pieces, testing decorative ideas, and generally making as much of a mess as you wish. No one will see it! In truth, these roughs can sometimes look better than the finished card if it is designed and decorated in an overly cautious way, so try to transfer some of the energy of the rough into the final version

Here is a rough of the Celebration pop-up next to the finished version. Although some of the ideas tried on the rough are used in the final design, many are rejected. Because a celebration with wine suggests a certain sophistication, the decoration was minimized and the color eliminated to make the card look stylish.

How To Make a Crease

There are three basic ways to make a crease: by hand, by scoring, or by indenting. Whichever method you choose will depend on the thickness of the paper or cardboard to be folded, and whether you are making a rough or a finished version. Everyone folds paper by hand, even if it is just to fold a letter in half, but if you are unfamiliar with scoring and indenting, it is wise to practice before making a pop-up.

By Hand

This method is possible only with thin or medium weight paper. It is generally very inaccurate and is recommended only for roughs of a pop-up, when speed is important and finesse is not!

1 Before folding, draw the folds on the paper.

2 Make each crease as a mountain-fold. Fold carefully along the drawn line.

3 Some of the mountain-folds may now need to be folded back on themselves to become valleys.

Scoring

Scoring is the best-known method for creasing thick paper and cardboard, but it is not entirely recommended. The fold is made by cutting through part of the thickness of the material, thus seriously weakening it. Nevertheless, scoring is useful when making roughs.

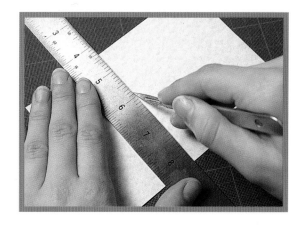

1 With a sharp blade and a steel rule, cut through about half the thickness of the paper of cardboard along the length of the fold on the mountain side.

2 Bend the card backwards to make the fold. Use care; if the cut is not made to exactly the right depth, the fold will be either too stiff or too floppy.

Indenting

Indenting is the best method for folding paper or cardboard of any thickness (except for mat board, which needs to be cut). The surface of the material is not cut, but compressed, thus preserving the full strength of the material along the fold.

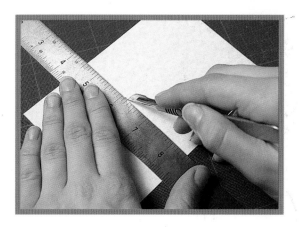

1 Turn a blade upside down, so that the blunt tip of the back of the blade is in contact with the paper or cardboard, then compress the material along the fold. Do not break the surface. Do this on the valley side the crease.

2 Bend the card forward to make the fold (the opposite way from when scoring). Compared to the scoring technique, the fold is much stronger.

How to Make a Backing Sheet

It is essential that the backing sheet on any pop-up is stiff, otherwise the pop-up structure will not fully open when the backing sheet is unfolded. To achieve this, the backing sheet is usually made from mat board, though sometimes a design will be strong enough if the backing sheet is made from thinner cardboard or thick paper.

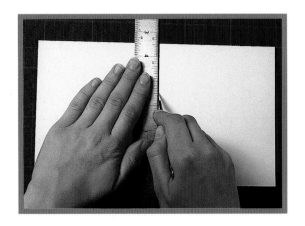

Here then is the method for making a backing sheet from mat board.

1 Cut out a piece of mat board to the size of the finished pop-up when it is opened flat. Draw a line down the center. Cut the card in two down the center line. Accuracy is important.

2 Lay one half over the other and trim off any excess to ensure that they are identical.

3 Butt the two halves up against each other and tape them together.

4 Turn the mat board over and neatly trim off the excess tape at both ends.

5 Turn over again. This is the basic backing sheet. However, it needs covering with a layer of medium weight paper to hide the tape and to coordinate the color of the backing sheet with the pop-up on top of it.

6 In a well-ventilated room or outdoors, spray adhesive on the backing sheet. Glue from a tube may also be used, but the spray is quicker and better.

7 Turn the glued backing sheet upside down and lower it onto the back of the covering layer of medium weight paper.

8 Trim off excess covering layer paper by carefully cutting around the edge of the mat board.

9 Turn over. Fold the backing sheet and covering layer in half and press firmly to make a sharp gutter crease down the center. This completes the backing sheet.

Fan Pop-Ups

Cartoon Explosion
The Cartoon Explosion project illustrates the fan pop-up technique and the drama of its 180-degree swivel.

Vase of Flowers
In the Vase of Flowers, the pink flower actually propels the "blooming" of the yellow flower.

Fan pop-ups are among the most dramatic and humorous of all pop-ups. This is primarily because the pop-up shape swivels through 180 degrees as the card is opened, to create movement. The technique is similar to that of the silhouette pop-up, in that both techniques create a "V" shape that straddles the gutter crease. Fan pop-ups, however, are not flat across the bottom (as are silhouette pop-ups) but are shallow "V" shapes themselves. This small change of angle creates a dramatic swiveling effect, though the angles themselves need to be calculated with precision if the effect is to work well. So, although fan pop-ups are simple and quick to create, they are subtle and need careful construction.

The two projects show different effects the fan design affords: Cartoon Explosion has an energetic, jagged outline, but the pop-up mechanism still works in the conventional way. In the Vase of Flowers, notice how the folds on the pink flower provide the power for the yellow flower to open, to create an unusual off-center pop-up effect. You could try adding a third flower, or even a fourth, each one being powered by the preceding one!

Fan Pop-Up Tips

- *Compare fan pop-ups with silhouette pop-ups. The difference is in the use of angles—in particular, the angle of the "V" across the gutter and the angle across the bottom of the pop-up.*
- *To learn how changing angles can affect the swiveling of a fan pop-up, spend fifteen minutes making a series of quick studies in which the angle of the "V" across the gutter and the angle across the bottom of the pop-up change in relation to each other.*
- *Accuracy in measuring angles is key; if your protractor is old and dirty, buy a new one—they are very inexpensive. If you are unfamiliar with how to use one, practice before making a pop-up.*

Materials

*For **Cartoon Explosion**, you will need*
- *Cartoon Explosion paper elements*
- *Thin white cardboard:*
  10" x 6" (25 cm x 15 cm) and
  8" x 5" (20 cm x 13 cm)

*For **Vase of Flowers**, you will need*
- *Vase of Flowers paper elements*
- *Sturdy backing sheet (see page 16):*
  8" x 7" (20 cm x 19 cm)
- *Covering layer: medium weight, soft pink paper, 8" x 7" (20 cm x 19 cm) or larger*

Equipment
- *Craft knife*
- *Glue*
- *Marker pens*
- *Pencil and eraser*
- *Protractor*
- *Ruler*

Cartoon Explosion

1 On the backing sheet, use a protractor to measure a very shallow "V" shape close to the top edge. The angle to each side of the gutter crease is 76 degrees. The paper elements and templates provide the correct angle for your convenience. Fold and unfold the gutter crease.

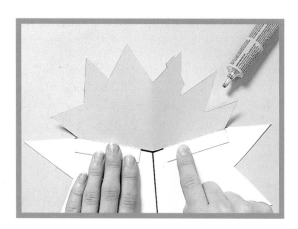

2 Glue the paper element tabs along the bottom edge of the pop-up to the line of the shallow "V." Note that the pop-up does not stand upright, but lies almost flat when the sheet is fully opened. Fold the backing sheet in half to check that the mechanism works well.

3 With a pencil, draw the explosion. For extra 3-D effect, allow "BANG!" to run from the backing sheet onto the pop-up and then right across it. Erase any unwanted lines.

4 Color in the explosion using bright marker pens—the gaudier it is, the better it will look! Use a black marker to outline some of the shapes.

Backing Sheet Shapes

This project proves that the gutter crease need not be in the middle of the backing sheet, and the backing sheet need not be rectangular—it can be any shape at all, however bizarre! Think hard about the shape of the backing sheet and where to place the gutter crease. The conventional rectangular backing sheet is often totally adequate, but to use backing sheets in a creative way can transform an ordinary design into something special. For further examples of irregular backing sheets and off-center gutter creases, look at the Locomotive, Car, and Photo Frame pop-ups.

Vase of Flowers

1 Cut out and fold the pink flower. Two mountain-folds and one valley-fold (folding from the back of the flower image) enable the flower to fold shut; if you are familiar with origami, this fold pattern will be recognized as a "waterbomb base."

2 Similarly, cut out and fold the yellow flower. If using the templates to create your own flowers, use the same medium weight, soft pink paper as on the covering layer. Collapse it shut along the folds. As with the previous flower, the angles between the folds are 45 degrees or 90 degrees. Measure them with a protractor, or if you are feeling confident, estimate them by eye.

3 Apply glue to the uncolored tab attached to the pink flower paper element. Lower the collapsed yellow flower onto the glue, such that the center point of the yellow flower touches the center fold on the pink one.

4 Now, collapse the pink flower shut, so that the other half of the glued tab sticks to the top surface of the yellow flower. Check the result against the photograph of the completed project.

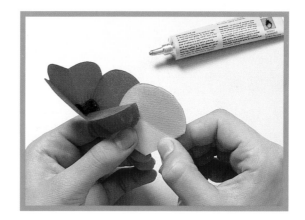

5 Make a sturdy backing sheet and covering layer. Draw the artwork, leaving a space where the pop-up flowers will be attached. The design is perhaps best created even before folding the flowers, so that the pop-up flowers and the design on the covering layer are well coordinated.

6 Apply glue to the underside of the pink flower paper element, then glue it to the covering layer as shown. The center point of the flower exactly touches the gutter, leaving angles of 45 degrees above and below it, to the right-hand side of the gutter. Then, apply glue to the top surface of the flower. Fold the backing sheet shut, so that it sticks to the glued surface. Unfold to reveal the finished design.

Fan Pop-Up Gallery

Top Hat

Like the Cartoon Explosion, the opening of the design sees the pop-up hat swivel dramatically into an upright position. Notice how the artwork carefully continues from the hat onto the head, so that the complete drawing is as convincing as possible.

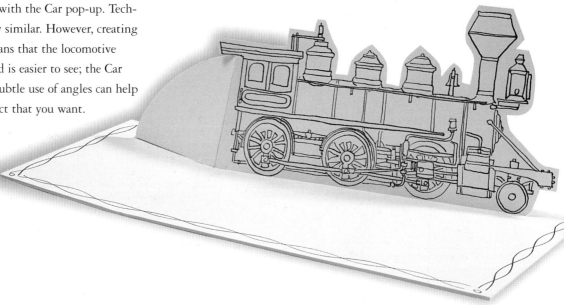

Locomotive

Compare this design with the Car pop-up. Technically, they look very similar. However, creating it as a fan pop-up means that the locomotive leans back a little, and is easier to see; the Car stands upright. The subtle use of angles can help create exactly the effect that you want.

Raspberry

The dramatic swiveling of the pop-up makes the fan technique perfect for humorous designs. Here, the tongue swivels downwards as the card opens.

Bookworm

Here, two fan pop-ups have been made: one for the book, the other for the reader. Notice that the reader is flatter that the book. This serves no technical purpose, but makes the design look a little more complex, and hence more interesting.

Songbird

Here, the pop-up has been placed low down on the gutter, so that it does not protrude much above the top edge of the backing sheet. The effect creates a restrained, quiet pop-up, helped by the sensitive use of colored pencil.

Silhouette Pop-Ups

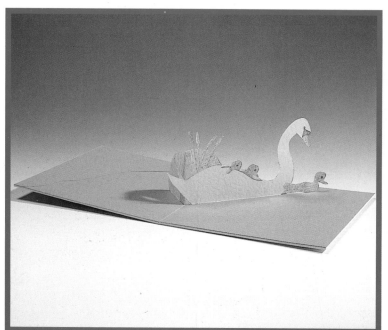

Swan and Cygnets
In Swan and Cygnets, the uncreased tail adds grace to the silhouette.

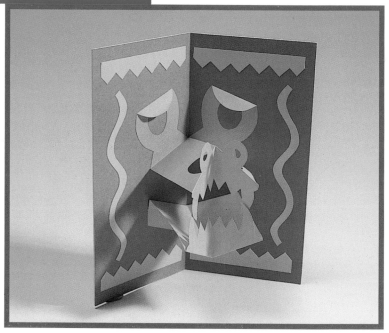

Monster Jaws
Monster Jaws does not open flat, but its effect is ferocious just the same.

T he silhoutte technique is probably the simplest and most versatile of all pop-up techniques. Constructions can be made with a minimal amount of simple measuring (even none at all, if you have the confidence to work freehand!) and the results can be very impressive. The pop-up can have any silhouette, however complex, and multiples can be arranged along the same gutter crease, as shown with the Dolphins and Cityscape ideas.

In Swan and Cygnets, notice how the tail of the swan is unfolded. It projects beyond the vertical fold to complete the graceful outline of the swan. When you design your own silhouette pop-ups, remember this useful device. It adds a lot of finesse.

The fun design of Monster Jaws really "snaps"! To make it work well, measure all the angles with great care—it helps to make a rough first. The backing sheet is not meant to open completely flat, so don't wrench it open with too much force. This design looks good when displayed, but it's seen at its best when held in the hand and played with.

Silhouette Pop-Up Tips

- *There are two ways to glue a silhouette pop-up to the backing sheet: cut slits in the backing sheet and tuck the tabs through, as in Swan and Cygnets, or glue the tabs of the paper elements on top of the backing sheet, as in Monster Jaws.*
- *The versatile silhouette technique lends itself to appealing asymmetric designs when the pop-up stands to one side of the mountain-fold that runs up the middle, as in Swan and Cygnets, Car, and Dolphins.*
- *Experiment with the angle of the "V" across the gutter crease. Sometimes the "V" can be very flat, sometimes it needs to be tighter. The tighter it is, the more stable the pop-up will become.*

Materials

*For **Swan and Cygnets**, you will need*
- *Swan and Cygnets paper elements*
- *Sturdy backing sheet (see page 16): 11" x 6" (27.5 cm x 15 cm)*
- *Covering layer: Medium weight blue paper, 11" x 6" (27.5 cm x 15 cm) or larger*

*For **Monster Jaws**, you will need*
- *Monster Jaws paper elements*
- *Sturdy backing sheet (see page 16): 7" x 7" (17.5 cm x 17.5 cm)*
- *Covering layer: Medium weight blue paper, 7" x 7" (17.5 cm x 17.5 cm) or larger*

Equipment
- *Craft knife*
- *Glue*
- *Colored pencils*
- *Pencil and eraser*
- *Protractor*
- *Spray adhesive*
- *Ruler*

Swan and Cygnets

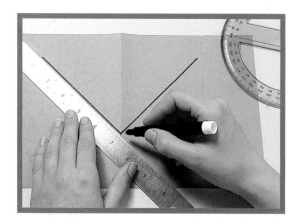

1 On the back of the covering layer, use a protractor to measure two 45-degree lines that meet at the gutter crease. Measure these angles with great care: if they are inaccurate, the pop-up will not close properly.

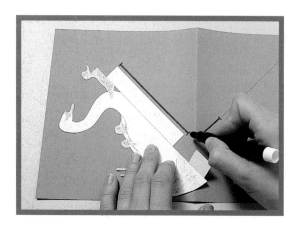

2 Cut out, fold, and color the swan and cygnets paper element. If creating a swan and cygnets from the templates, use textured, medium weight white paper. On the "V" lines on the covering layer, draw darker lines that exactly coincide with the position of the tabs on the pop-up.

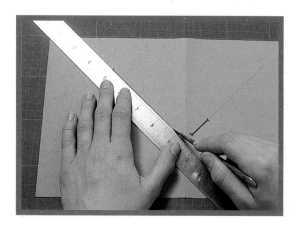

3 Cut along the dark lines. Note that because this is the back of the covering layer, the long and short lines that represent the position of the tabs are the reverse of how they will appear when the covering layer is turned over and seen from the front. It is annoyingly easy to position the tabs the wrong way—back-to-front—so think through this step very carefully when designing your own pop-ups.

4 On the front, push the tabs through the slits. Glue or tape them into position on the back. This is the point when you discover if the correct length of slit made in step 3 is on the correct side of the gutter crease. In pop-ups, planning is everything!

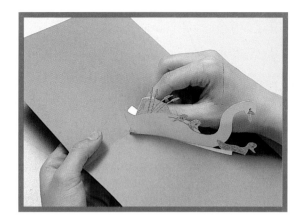

5 Make a sturdy backing sheet. Cover the front with an even layer of spray adhesive.

6 Fold the covering layer in half. Lay the gutter crease on the covering layer exactly over the gutter crease on the backing sheet. This is a little awkward to do, but the spray adhesive will allow you to pull the covering layer off and reposition it.

7 Fold the backing sheet in half so that it glues itself to the top of the covering layer. Open out the pop-up. If it will not open flat, fold it in half again and reposition the covering layer so that it is better aligned with the backing sheet. Once everything is perfect, trim off the excess covering layer paper to tidy up the final design.

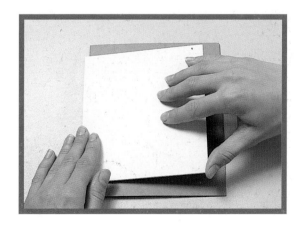

Monster Jaws

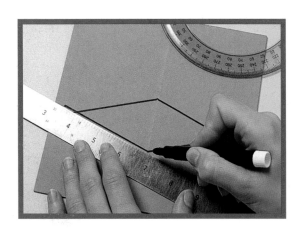

1 Make a sturdy backing sheet and covering layer. Trim off excess covering layer paper. Draw two "V" shapes, 2" (5 cm) apart, each arm creating an angle of 70 degrees to the gutter crease. Note that this 70-degree angle is the same as the angle on the two jaw pieces. This parity ensures that the jaws will "snap."

2 Cut out and fold the upper jaw paper element as shown. If you create the jaw pieces from the templates, use medium weight pink paper for both pieces. Note how the nostrils project above the level of the "V" crease, and how the tops of the eyes fold over to create eyebrows. Simple effects such as these add interest to a pop-up, particularly as they are achieved without decorating the paper with felt pens, colored pencils, or crayons.

3 Apply glue to the back surface of the eyes, then glue them to the covering layer. The "V" crease that runs along the bottom of the eyes must lie along the top "V" crease on the covering layer. To achieve this, the jaw piece must be flattened against the covering layer.

4 Fold the backing sheet in half, allowing the jaw to swing forwards and upwards. When the backing sheet is folded flat in half, press it very hard to reinforce the creases on the jaw piece.

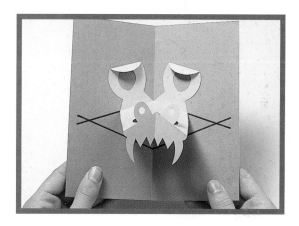

5 Cut out and fold the lower jaw paper element. Note that it is essentially the same shape as the upper jaw, though simpler. Apply glue to the back of the paper element tabs.

6 The lower jaw cannot be glued to the covering layer in the same way as the upper jaw (by being pressed flat against the covering layer), because the upper jaw is now in the way. So, although it's awkward, lower one glued tab onto the covering layer as shown, lining up the crease with the line drawn on the backing sheet. Then, begin to fold the backing sheet in half, so that the second glued tab sticks to the opposite half of the covering layer, up against the other side of the gutter crease. The effect is the same as the upper jaw, but upside down.

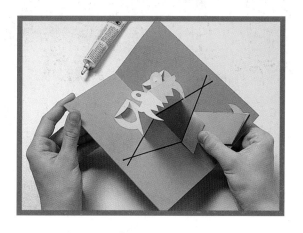

Silhouette Pop-Up Gallery

Airliner

The silhouette technique is wonderful for dramatically lifting a pop-up high above the backing sheet. Remember to reinforce the vertical stake by doubling or trebling the thickness of the paper—a single layer will flop to one side.

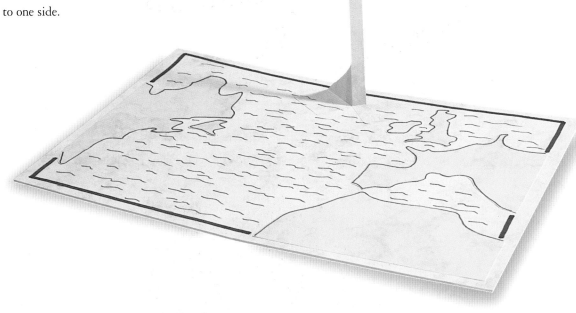

Car

When the pop-up stands to one side of the gutter crease (as the car does here), the backing sheet on the other side of the gutter can seem very large and very empty. The solution is to reduce it in size, so that the gutter becomes off-center.

Cityscape

Layer upon layer of "V" shapes of paper can be laid across the gutter crease to create elaborate multi-layered designs. A cityscape is a natural subject for this treatment, but you could also design a landscape, jungle, or desert in the same way. Notice how the layers become taller toward the back.

Puppies

In this design, the "V" shape recedes rather than advances, so the pop-up is at the front of the card, not at the back. The effect gives the puppies greater prominence. For added visual interest, the small dog bowl points forward.

Entwined Hearts

This spectacular pop-up is actually very easy to make. The "V" of paper that crosses the gutter crease is enclosed across the back to make a box that is technically identical to the Movie Theatre project. Here, though, the back hearts slot into the front hearts—no glue is used.

Tent Pop-Ups

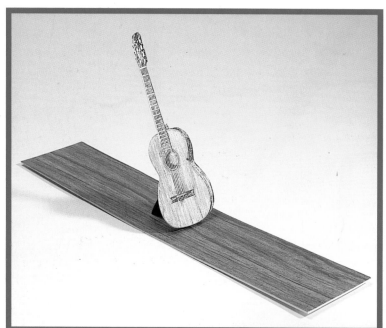

Guitar

The Guitar uses the basic tent technique.

Stars

Stars incorporates an unusual twist, with the two stars sharing a fold.

It could be said that the tent technique is the silhouette technique "turned upright." They are fundamentally similar, yet achieve different pop-up effects. The technique is also a relative of the scenery flats technique, in that both display a flat pop-up shape on the front of a supporting tab.

The guitar project shows the basic tent technique. Once learned, it can be used to display any shape with any silhouette, or even be turned sideways, as in the Balloon idea at the end of the chapter. Simple, versatile, and particularly good at displaying objects in a seemingly unsupported way, the tent technique creates a feeling of lightness that is unusual in a pop-up. In the Stars project, the ingenious way in which the two stars are joined by a fold is an unusual but effective use of tent technique. To make more stars, simply continue the joining pattern and make a longer gutter crease.

Tent Pop-Up Tips

- *The supporting tab behind the main pop-up is best made so that it slots through the covering layer. In this way, its glue tabs are hidden out of sight and the final design looks much tidier.*

- *Note how some of the projects (Stars) and gallery pop-ups (Clothesline, Eiffel Tower, Campsite, Easel) use the basic tent form as part of the final design, whereas others (Guitar, Balloon, Photo Frame) hide it behind a flat cut-out.*

- *If you are looking for an elegant technical challenge, try making the Guitar and Stars projects from a single sheet of stiff cardboard, instead of from separate pieces. The pop-up shapes are cut from the backing sheet, lifted upright along folds where folds are currently made, and glued together over the gutter.*

Materials

For **Guitar**, you will need
- *Guitar paper elements*
- *Sturdy backing sheet (see page 16): 14" x 3" (35 cm x 7.5 cm)*
- *Covering layer: Wood-grain shelf paper, 14" x 3" (35 cm x 7.5 cm) or larger*
- *Support: Shelf paper, 5" x 1" (12.5 cm x 2.5 cm)*

For **Stars**, you will need
- *Stars paper elements*
- *Sturdy backing sheet (see page 16): 11" x 6" (28 cm x 15 cm)*
- *Covering layer: Medium weight red paper, 11" x 6" (28 cm x 15 cm) or larger*

Equipment

Craft knife
Glue
Colored pencils
Pencil and eraser
Pair of compasses
Ruler
Protractor
Gold marker pen (optional)

Guitar

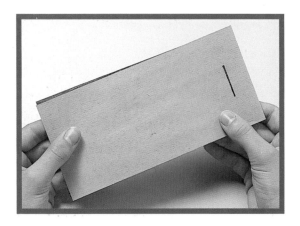

1 Fold the covering layer in half. Draw a line 1" (2.5 cm) long, ³/₄" (2 cm) away from the gutter crease. The length of the line will match the width of the supporting tab. Its distance from the gutter dictates how upright the tab will stand—the closer to the gutter it is, the more vertical the tab will be.

2 Cut along the drawn line through both layers. Make sure that the cut is exactly parallel to the gutter crease. Cutting through both layers at once guarantees that the construction will be symmetrical.

3 Open the covering layer. Cut out and fold the support from the guitar paper elements. Push the tabs through the slits on the covering layer and glue or tape them in place underneath.

4 Make a sturdy backing sheet. Spray the front surface with an even layer of spray adhesive.

5 With great care, lower the folded covering layer onto the backing sheet, so that the gutter crease on the covering layer is exactly on top of the crease on the backing sheet. Take as much time as you need to do this perfectly.

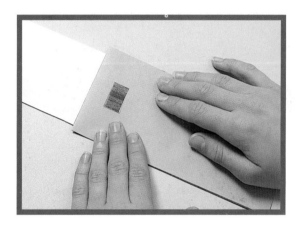

6 Close the backing sheet onto the other half of the covering layer. Open the pop-up and trim the excess covering layer paper. If the backing sheet will not open flat, this is probably because the covering layer was not positioned accurately at step 5, so reposition it—the spray adhesive allows you to do this.

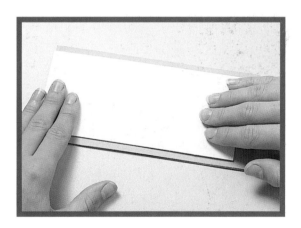

7 Cut out the guitar paper element. If you make the guitar from the template, use thin cardboard. Apply glue to the front of the supporting tab and fix the guitar to it; if the shape is particularly large or spindly, reinforce it with an extra layer of cardboard. Here, the guitar neck has an extra layer glued to it to prevent it from bending backwards over a period of time.

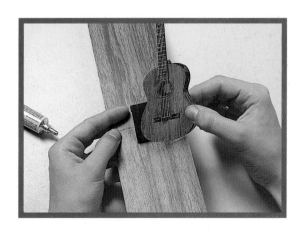

Stars

1 Cut out the Stars paper elements, or follow the templates and make your own from thin white card rather than paper (so that the stars will be sturdy).

2 On a sheet of medium weight red paper, the same size or a little larger than the sturdy backing sheet, draw a central gutter crease. Then, 3" (8 cm) away from the crease on each side, draw four short lines to coincide with the position of the tabs on the stars' feet. Cut along the four lines. Note that this is the back of the sheet, so position the cuts the reverse of how they would be on the front side.

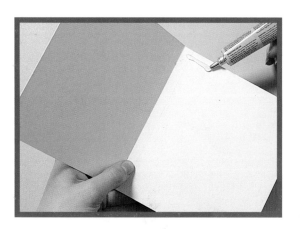

3 Make an 11" x 6" (28 cm x 15 cm) sturdy backing sheet, but do not cover the card with paper. Apply glue to the front.

4 With great care, lower the glued surface of the backing sheet onto the colored layer of paper, so that the two center creases exactly align. Take your time and do this perfectly.

5 Trim off the excess paper to create a tidy edge to the backing sheet. This can be done without a ruler: the thickness of the card will keep your knife running straight.

6 Carefully push the tabs on the stars into the slits made in step 2. This will be made easier if, back in step 3, glue is not applied around the tab areas. When the feet are all securely inserted, fold the whole card in half to finally create the gutter crease through the colored layer.

Tent Pop-Up Gallery

Balloon

The supporting tab used to support the Guitar may also be used with the backing sheet standing upright, so that a shape (here, a balloon) can apparently hang suspended in mid-air. Compare this design with the Celebration project—it is technically similar, but simpler.

Photo Frame

This is indeed an eccentric design: the pop-up is bigger than the backing sheet. Nevertheless, this simple project is a wonderful way to send an important photograph to someone, so that they may easily display it. A larger backing sheet would make the overall design look clumsy. The photograph rests on a support similar to that in the Guitar.

Eiffel Tower

This is one of the simplest pop-ups to make, yet quite dramatic. Two images of the Eiffel Tower are glued to the backing sheet astride the gutter and glued together at the top.

Campsite

The tent features a conventional support with an extra triangle glued across the middle to create the front flap of the tent. A fold down the center of the triangle allows it to collapse when the backing sheet is closed shut. The flagpole is glued to the gutter crease.

Clothesline

Cotton thread is a material that is underused in pop-ups. It has many interesting technical uses, and it creates a satisfying airiness that contrasts well with conventional solid blocks of paper or cardboard.

Box Pop-Ups

Gift Box

This square-on box pop-up sits directly on the gutter crease.

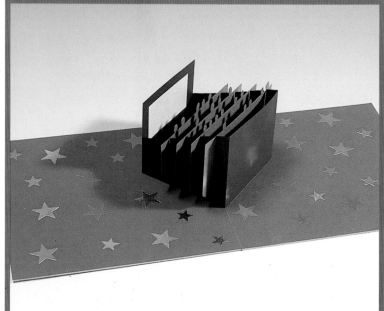

Movie Theater

Movie Theater uses the diagonal box pop-up structure.

There are two main box pop-up techniques: the "square-on" box, which sits squarely over the gutter crease, and the "diagonal box," which sits at 45 degrees across the gutter. These techniques are popular because they convey a sense of solidity and completeness. They are also wonderful to watch when the backing sheet is opened and closed. Even the smallest error will mean that a 3-D box will not collapse flat, so take as much time as you need to construct a design—it will be very helpful to make an accurate rough.

When building the Gift Box, you will find that a completely solid pop-up is a particularly satisfying structure to make, because the way that it erects and flattens as the backing sheet opens and closes is fascinating to watch. With the Movie Theater, the "diagonal box" version of the Box technique can look somewhat uninteresting just as a square tube, so this design introduces four panels that cross the box in parallel. The result is a design complex in shape, but simple in concept.

Box Pop-Up Tips

- *The "square-on" box technique is constructed from several pieces, so check and double-check that, where applicable, measurements on different pieces that are meant to be the same are precisely so. Do this before gluing them together.*

- *Don't let your concentration slip! With both techniques, it is easy to concentrate on the construction of the boxes, and forget about the covering layer. The covering layer must be measured and cut with the same precision as the boxes.*

- *Try constructing hexagonal boxes, or cylinders, or making a lid for the diagonal box. The box principle is a surprisingly creative one and many elegant forms can be constructed with a little experimentation. Try making other solids too, such as a pyramid.*

Materials

*For **Gift Box**, you will need*

- *Gift Box paper elements*
- *Sturdy backing sheet (see page 16): 8" x 5" (20 cm x 13 cm)*
- *Covering layer: Medium weight green paper, 8" x 5 ¹/₂" (20 cm x 14 cm) or larger*
- *Brown wrapping paper: Approx. 19" x 8" (48 cm x 20 cm)*

*For **Movie Theater**, you will need*

- *Movie Theater paper elements*
- *Sturdy backing sheet (see page 16): 13" x 6 ¹/₂" (33 cm x 16.5 cm)*
- *Covering layer: Medium weight red paper, 13" x 6 ¹/₂" (33 cm x 16.5 cm) or larger*

Equipment

Craft knife

Glue

Colored pencils

Pencil and eraser

Protractor

Ruler

Air mail stickers (optional)

Gummed gold and silver stars (optional)

Gift Box

1 Make two slits in a sheet of medium weight green paper at least 8" x 5 ½" (20 cm x 14 cm), the size of the sturdy backing sheet. Each slit is 2 ½" (6 cm) long and 1" (2.5 cm) away from the gutter crease.

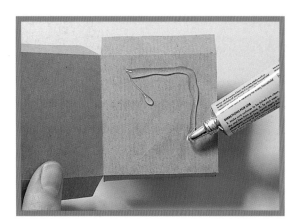

2 Cut out the Gift Box paper elements. Fold the support as shown on the paper element. Apply glue to one of the large panels, then fold it in half to glue it tight shut. Make sure that all the edges and folds align.

3 Glue the support to the gutter crease, centered between the two cuts. Fold the support flat against the backing sheet and check that the edges of the support line up with the ends of the cuts.

4 Apply glue to the tabs across the top of the support. Lower the lid onto the tabs, being careful to exactly align the fold on the lid with the edge along the top of the support.

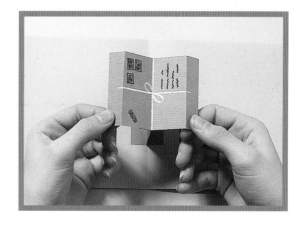

5 Fold the paper element that will become the walls of the box. Glue the tab at one end of the strip to the other end, to make a square tube. Push the bottom tabs through the cuts in the backing sheet, and secure them beneath with tape or glue.

6 Apply glue to the two tabs on the lid. Glue the tabs to the sides of the box, making sure that they are positioned exactly in line with the top edge.

7 Fold the backing sheet in half. Apply glue to two 5 ¹/₂" x 4" (14 cm x 10 cm) rectangles of mat board and glue them to the backing sheet, one on each side of the gutter crease. Trim off the excess colored paper.

Movie Theater

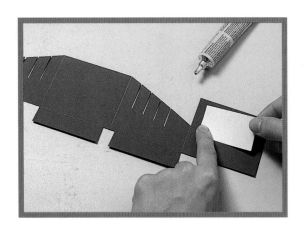

1 Cut out the Movie Theater paper elements. If you're creating your own from the templates, make the theater from thin blue cardboard, the audience from thin grey cardboard, and the screen from medium weight paper. Glue the movie screen to the larger theater piece. The example shown here is white, but you may use a still from a real movie. The accurate cutting of this piece is very important, as any inaccuracy will be seen against the dark background.

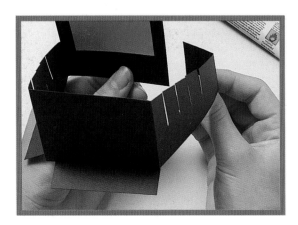

2 Fold the theater piece along all the folds shown on the paper element. Glue the end tab behind the screen to make a square tube. If the tube can squash flat, everything is perfectly aligned; if it will not squash flat, adjust the position of the tab behind the screen. Remember, if the piece will not flatten, neither will the completed pop-up.

3 This is the completed theater piece. If it has been incorrectly measured and no amount of repositioning of the end tab will allow it to flatten, you unfortunately have no alternative but to make it again. Before doing so, check the measurements to find the error, so that when it is remade, you will know what to correct.

4 On the covering layer, draw two lines at 45 degrees to the gutter crease, which meet about 2 ½" (6 cm) from the top edge of the covering layer. The angles must be exactly equal, so double-check them with a protractor before proceeding to the next step.

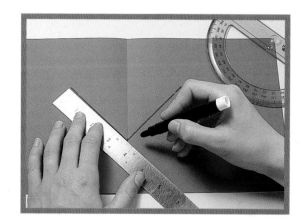

5 Position the tabs on the large theater piece over the top of the drawn lines. Mark on the lines where the tabs begin and end. Note the small gap across the gutter between the marked lines.

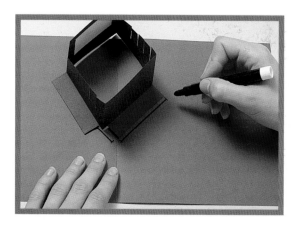

6 Cut along both marked lines with a knife. It is probably a good idea to exceed the length of the lines by a fraction. This will ensure that the tabs will have a little slack when inserted. Too much slack, though, will leave an unsightly cut on the covering layer—so lengthen the slit with discretion.

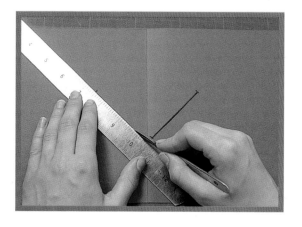

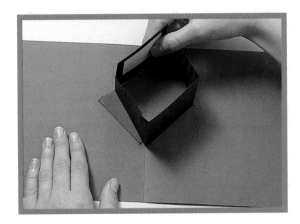

7 Insert the tabs through the slits. If the fit is very tight, lengthen the slits a little rather than risk tearing the covering layer. Slip the tabs in position on the underside of the covering layer, securing with tape or glue.

8 Make a sturdy backing sheet. Cover the front with an even layer of spray adhesive, remembering to do this in a well-ventilated room, or outdoors.

9 Fold the covering layer in half, allowing the theater piece to collapse flat inside. Lower the covering layer onto one half of the backing sheet, so that the gutter on the covering layer exactly follows the line of the gutter on the backing sheet. Do this with considerable care. Fold the remaining half of the backing sheet over the top so that it sticks to the top of the covering layer. Unfold to check that everything has worked well, then trim off the excess covering layer paper.

10 Cut out the four audience panels. Each piece contains two slits exactly 3" (6.5 cm) apart and half the height of the panel. Each panel is a different height and equal in height to its position within the theater against the sloping side walls. Thus, each piece needs measuring independently and with care.

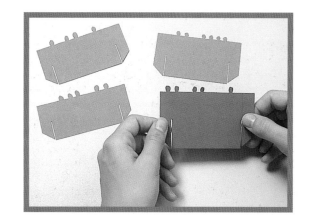

11 Slot each panel into position. Note that the slits in the theater piece and audience are not the width of a single knife cut, but are wider, made with two slits just a fraction apart. These wide slits help the structure to swivel flat when the backing sheet is closed. Note the stars on the covering layer, added for decoration.

12 Test the accuracy of the construction by folding the design in half. The audience panels will swivel flat in an elegant and fascinating way! If the swiveling is a little sticky, check the measurements on the audience panels, particularly the 3" (6.5 cm) distance between the slits on each piece, and the width of each slit (see step 11).

Box Pop-Up Gallery

Ruined Temple

The same boxes made in the Movie Theater and the Cactus can easily be stretched to become rectangular boxes. Also, the simple outlines of those two boxes can be made very complex. The Ruined Temple is a rectangular box with a complex silhouette.

Tic-Tac-Toe Game

This design may be a little whimsical, but it is nevertheless a very practical idea! The support for the game board is similar to the Gift Box, but without the solid faces across the middle—they are unnecessary. All manner of board games could be presented in this way, perhaps on a large scale.

Picture Frame

A favorite photograph, postcard, or magazine image can form the picture, and the frame can be as ornate as you wish. Don't lift the picture too far away from the backing sheet on tall supports, or it will sag.

Puppet Theater

The Movie Theater box is adapted to make a traditional toy puppet theater. Different scenery flats may be slotted into place to create different backdrops for the action. The figures move left and right on slats of thick cardboard. Try making a big puppet theater at least 2' (60 cm) across, using very stiff cardboard.

Cactus

The four arms of the cactus are slotted into the four sides of the box that straddles the valley-fold. The box itself is a simplified version of the Movie Theater project. Two pieces of cardboard are slotted together to make the cactus. Thus, although complex, the design uses very little glue.

Coil Pop-Ups

Coil Heart
The Coil Heart project shows what can be done with a simple application of the coil technique.

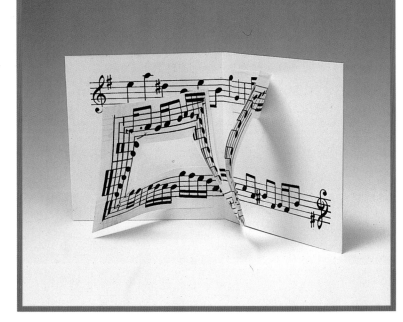

Musical Score
The Musical Score is a bit more complex.

The coil technique is a curious one: it requires little or no measuring, and no careful construction, and the final result is often apparently nongeometric, even haphazard. The result can appear so random that to the uninitiated, even the simplest coil can seem clever. The only technical subtlety is to know how many revolutions the coil should have: too few and the backing sheet will not open fully flat; too many and the coil will flop about and not stretch open. As a general rule, between two and three revolutions should be about right, depending upon whether the ends are glued to the backing sheet near to or far from the valley-fold.

The Coil Heart, a pleasingly simple and quick-to-make design, is good for beginners because the pop-up mechanism is very reliable and requires no measuring. The Musical Score differs from the other step-by-step coil designs in the chapter because the coil does not spiral inward to a point of origin, but remains a constant width, rather like a spiral staircase.

Coil Pop-Up Tips

- *Learn the basic technical difference between the flat, simple one-piece coil used to make the Coil Heart and the multiple-piece coil used to make the Musical Score. Once the difference is understood, many different pop-ups can be made.*

- *In the rough, experiment with gluing the coils to different places on the backing sheet. In some positions, the coil will barely open; in others, it will twist awkwardly. Seek the place where it stretches just right and looks balanced.*

- *Try combining the coil technique with others. For example, use it between a silhouette or tent pop-up and the backing sheet, or between a scenery flat and the backing sheet. The results can look spectacular and bizarre!*

Materials

*For **Coil Heart**, you will need*
- *Coil Heart paper elements*
- *Sturdy backing sheet (see page 16): 11" x 5" (28 cm x 13 cm)*
- *Covering layer: Medium weight yellow paper, 11" x 5" (28 cm x 13 cm)*

*For **Musical Score**, you will need*
- *Musical Score paper elements*
- *Sturdy backing sheet (see page 16): 11" x 6" (28 cm x 15 cm)*
- *Covering layer: copy paper, 11" x 6" (28 cm x 15 cm)*
- *Coil: Enough photocopies of lines of music to make 14 pieces, each 5" x 1 1/2" (13 cm x 4 cm)*

Equipment

Craft knife
Glue
Ruler
Photocopier

Coil Heart

1 Make an 11" x 5" (28 cm x 13 cm) sturdy backing sheet.

2 Cut out the blue coil heart paper element, or create one using the templates and medium weight blue paper. Hold it so that the spiral coils counterclockwise from the edge to the center, then glue the end as shown.

3 Turn the coil over so that the glue is on the underside. Glue the coil into position on the backing sheet to the right of the gutter.

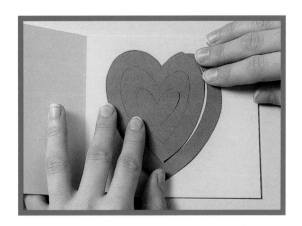

4 Glue the top surface at the center of the heart. Be careful not to let the glue spread beyond the center.

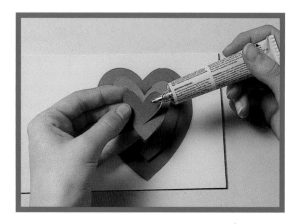

5 Fold the backing sheet in half, so that the center of the heart glues onto the left-hand half of the backing sheet.

6 Open the backing sheet to see the blue heart uncoiling across the gutter. Cut out the red heart paper element—or make one using the template and medium weight red paper—and glue it onto the coils, so that it is prominently displayed.

Musical Score

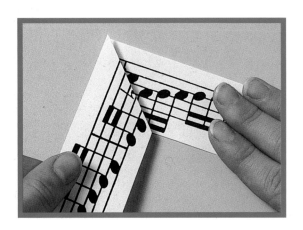

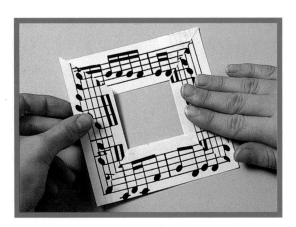

1 Cut out paper elements. Glue two pieces together as shown, ensuring that the angle between them is exactly 90 degrees. If you are using the paper templates to make this pop-up, make sure you you cut out twelve of the beveled shape and two of the rectangle shape.

2 Continue the pattern, gluing the third and fourth pieces into position. Once again, create exact 90-degree angles at the corners.

3 Glue together a total of seven pieces to form this square-section coil. The seventh piece is one of the two rectangular paper elements, used to create a flat end to the coil.

4 Turn the coil over. Glue the remaining seven units exactly onto the back of the first seven so that the musical score runs along both sides of the coil.

5 This is the completed coil. If the back-to-back gluing of the pieces looks a little ragged, trim the edges to neaten the effect.

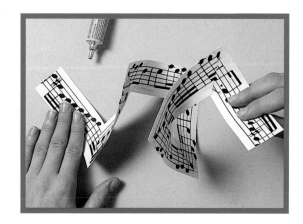

6 Make a sturdy backing sheet. For the covering layer, two additional rectangular lines of music have been supplied. Place them an exact distance apart. That distance is the same as the distance between the lines of music along opposite edges of the square coil.

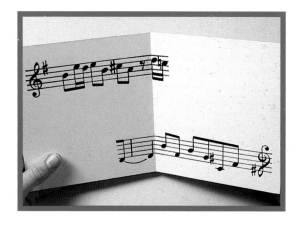

7 Glue one end of the coil to the backing sheet, so that the music flows uninterrupted across the join. Then glue the top surface of the other end of the coil and close the backing sheet over it, so that the glued end sticks to the backing sheet. If your measurements at step 6 were accurate, the music at this end of the coil will exactly join up with the music on the backing sheet.

Coil Pop-Up Gallery

Fireworks

The three firework rockets are glued to those parts of coils that
stand vertically, so that the rockets themselves will also stand
vertically, like the Coil Heart. The bright colors were achieved
with oil pastel and glitter.

Soccer Kick

Again, this design is essentially the same as the Aerobatic Plane. If soccer isn't an appropriate sport to depict, adapt the image to one that is more relevant, such as football, baseball, golf, cricket, volleyball, and so on.

Rollercoaster

This is essentially the same as the Aerobatic Plane, but with fewer rotations of the coil. Try changing the shape of the coil to achieve a different corkscrew effect, perhaps to mimic a real ride in a real theme park.

Aerobatic Plane

A pop-up design need not always stand up on a horizontal surface such as a desk or shelf. When appropriate to the design, it could hang on a wall! The coil here is similar to the square-sectioned coil used to make the Musical Score, but it's circular and thus requires considerably fewer pieces to make.

Scenery Flats Pop-Ups

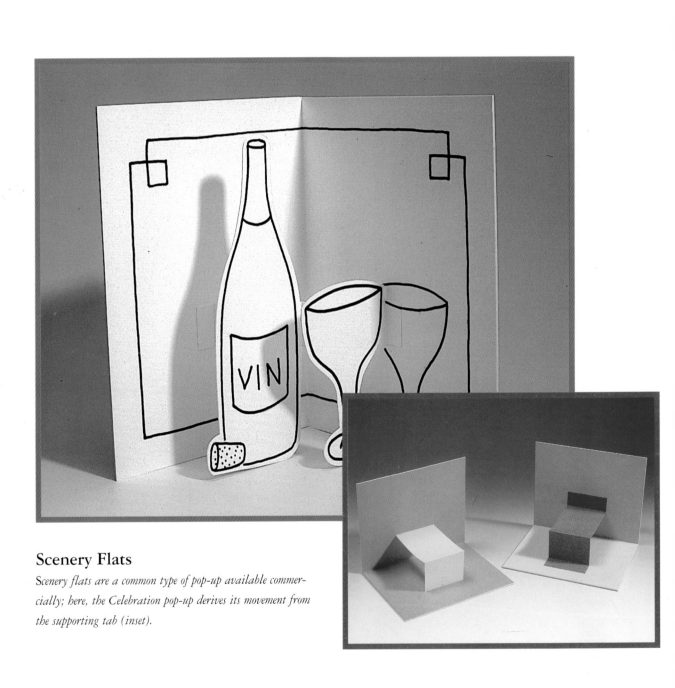

Scenery Flats

Scenery flats are a common type of pop-up available commercially; here, the Celebration pop-up derives its movement from the supporting tab (inset).

A long with the silhouette technique, the scenery flats technique is probably the most widely used in commercially produced pop-up books and greeting cards. The reason for this is not hard to see: it creates any number of seemingly unsupported flat shapes that stand behind or beside each other to make appealingly complex pop-up designs.

Ironically, the most important part of the technique is rarely seen—the supporting tab. The measuring and placement of the tab on the covering layer is critical and must be understood before the scenery flats technique can be used with any fluency. If you are able to make these tabs accurately, all manner of wonderful designs can be created. However, each tab must be measured and constructed with great care.

Materials

*For **Celebration**, you will need*
- *Celebration paper elements*
- *Sturdy backing sheet (see page 16):*
  12" x 8" (30 cm x 20 cm)
- *Covering layer: thick white paper,*
  12" x 8" (30 cm x 20 cm) or larger

Equipment
- *Craft knife*
- *Glue*
- *Black marker pen*
- *Pencil and eraser*
- *Ruler*

Scenery Flats Pop-Up Tips

- *Make the supporting tab exercise suggested on the next spread, then make a few more with different measurements for extra practice. This may seem a little pedantic, but learning the technique well will save you time later when you design your own pop-ups.*

- *In the pop-up gallery, the Golfer combines the scenery flats technique with the silhouette technique. Consider also combining the technique with tent or box techniques—they both make excellent backgrounds for supporting tabs.*

- *Remember that if scenery flats are designed with too many layers, one behind another connected by supporting tabs, the layers at the front will not be pulled fully upright by the layers behind. As a general rule, four layers is the maximum—any more and the construction may begin to wilt at the front.*

How to Make a Supporting Tab

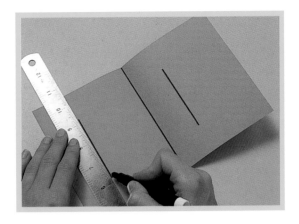

1 On a covering layer of medium weight paper, approximately 9" x 6" (22.5 cm x 15 cm), draw a central gutter crease. Draw a line to each side of the valley. For this exercise, the two lines are exactly 3" (8 cm) and 1 ½" (4 cm) upon the design that you are making.

2 Make a supporting tab from medium weight paper. The distances between the creases must be exactly the same as those measured on the covering layer: 3" and 1 ½" (8 cm and 4 cm). Include a glue tab at each end, beyond the creases. For this exercise, the width of the tab is 2" (5 cm).

3 Place the end folds on the supporting tab exactly over the lines drawn on the covering layer. Mark the lines on the covering layer where the edge of the tab crosses them.

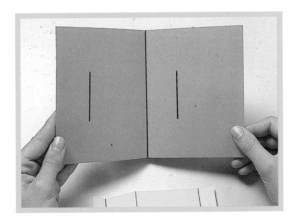

4 Here are the lines between the marks made in step 3. The length of each line should be the width of the supporting tab.

5 Cut each line, checking first that they are exactly parallel to the valley-fold. In fact, you may wish to cut a fraction beyond the ends of each line, in order to help the glue tabs push through in step 6 without risk of tearing the covering layer paper if the fit is too tight.

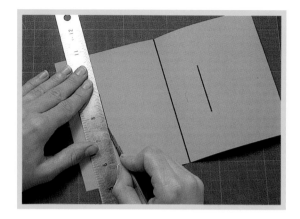

6 This is the step that can confuse! The glue tabs at the ends of the supporting tabs are pushed through the slits in the covering layer, but which tab goes through which slit? The rule is that the glue tab *nearer* the mountain-fold on the supporting tab is pushed through the slit *further* away from the valley-fold. This is the opposite to how you might imagine it.

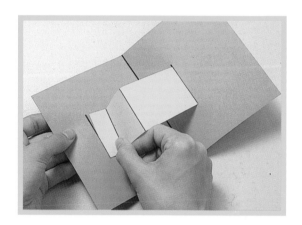

7 Glue the glue tabs to the back of the supporting layer. Note that the mountain-fold on the supporting tab does not lie on top of the valley-fold on the covering layer. Instead, it lies to one side. It looks wrong, but it isn't.

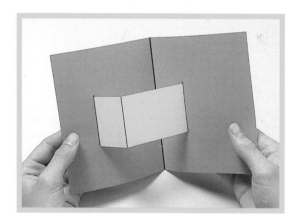

8 For extra strength, glue the covering layer to a sturdy backing sheet. When designing a rough, instead of carefully making slits to hide the glue tabs, just glue the tabs to the front of the covering layer. The pink and red example shows this time-saving alternative.

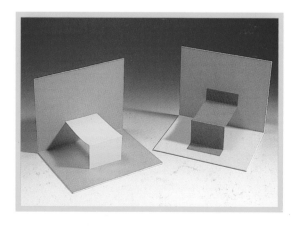

Celebration

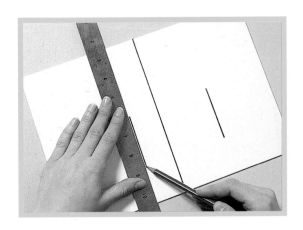

1 Make a sturdy backing sheet, then put a covering layer of thick white paper over it. Draw two lines parallel to the gutter, 2 ³/₄" (6.5 cm) away on the right, and 1 ¹/₂" (4 cm) away on the left.

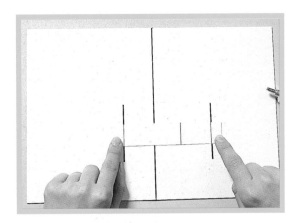

2 Cut out the strap paper elements, or create them with the templates and thick white paper. Glue the tabs at both ends of the large strap, then glue the strap flat to the backing sheet, creasing it first. The bottom edge of the strap is 2 ¹/₂" (4 cm) away from the bottom edge of the backing sheet. Note that the mountain-fold is to the right of the gutter crease, not in line with it.

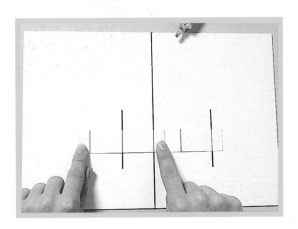

3 Similarly, fold the small tab, then glue the tabs at both ends. Glue it flat, so that the left tab glues to the backing sheet and the right tab glues onto the large strap. Note that the right-hand fold is in line with the gutter.

4 This is the three-dimensional result of steps 1 through 3. Fold the card in half and press it flat to strengthen all the creases. Some of them may move a fraction, but don't worry!

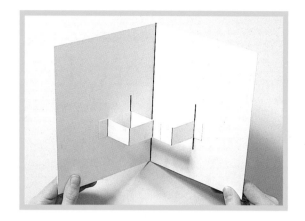

5 Draw the background illustration on the backing sheet. If your card is to have a greeting or message, add it now.

6 Cut out the glass and bottle paper elements, or create them from thick white paper using the templates. Glue the bottle and glass to the two right-facing straps. Be careful to line up the bottom of the bottle and glass with the bottom edge of the card, so that they appear to stand on the same surface as the card.

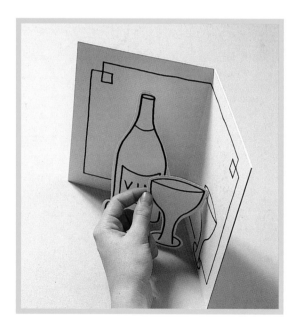

Scenery Flats Pop-Up Gallery

Speech Bubbles

Each bubble is held away from the backing sheet by its own supporting tab. For extra interest, the bubbles are fixed to opposite faces of the tabs, so that they face in opposite directions.

Chair

Chairs, sofas, and tables make excellent subjects for the student of the scenery flats technique to study, because they are simply a series of linked supporting tabs, each built on a predecessor. Many ingenious designs can be created, some very elaborate. As a variation, try designing the same chair, but this time turned sideways against the backing sheet.

Tea Time

Similar to the Celebration project, this design features three scenery flat pieces: the teapot, cup, and cake-stand. The teapot is fixed to a supporting tab; the cake-stand is fixed to the teapot at one end and has its own integral tab on the right to fix it to the backing sheet; the cup is fixed directly to the cake-stand at one end and to the pot by a tab at the other end. In this way, all the pieces are attached to each other or to the backing sheet.

Woodland Glade

Elaborate, multilayered scenes can be designed with much playfulness once the method for constructing the supporting tab is understood. Note how each scenery flat piece is connected to the one behind by means of a tab, until the furthest back connects to the background by means of a final tab.

Golfer

A supporting tab always needs fixing at one end to a vertical surface and at the other to a horizontal one. A silhouette pop-up stood on a backing sheet meets these requirements and is an excellent way to support a scenery flat (here, the golfer). Other supporting tabs could be fixed to the same silhouette background, perhaps on the other side of the valley.

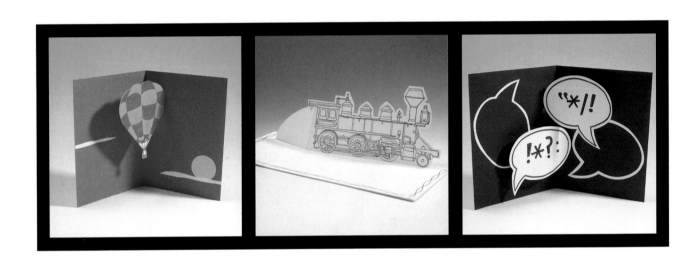

About the Author

Paul Jackson is a professional paper artist and paper engineer who has an M.A. in Fine Art from the University of London. He has written many books on pop-ups, origami, and paper sculpture, and lectures at art and design schools in the United Kingdom, Europe, and the United States. Jackson makes models commissioned by advertising agencies and design companies, and he exhibits widely.

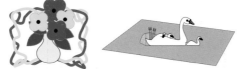

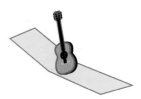

Paper Elements and Templates

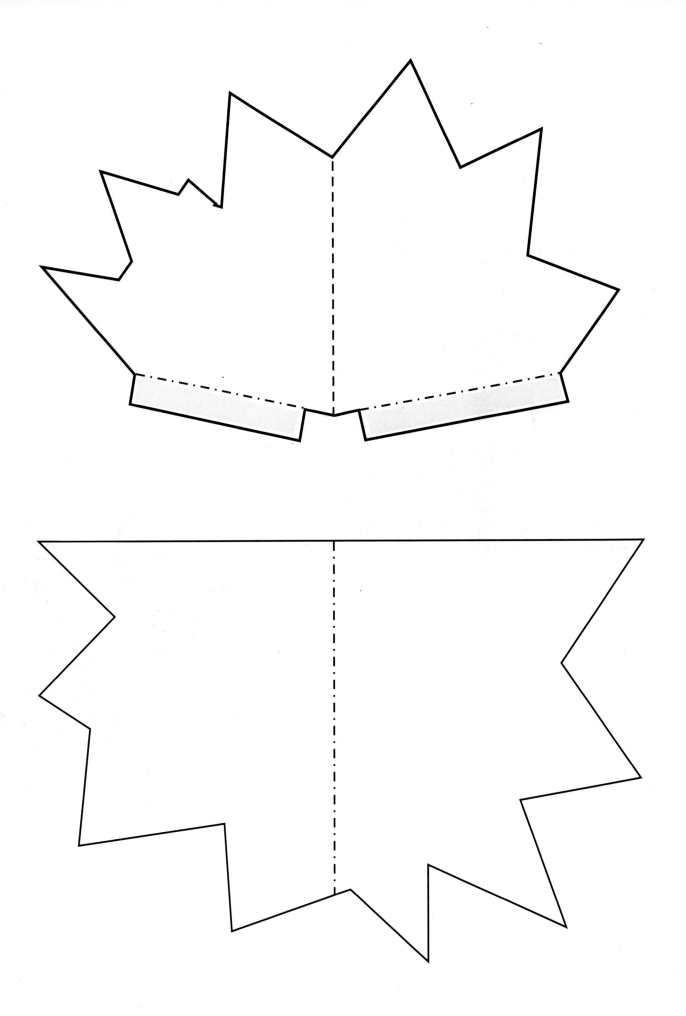

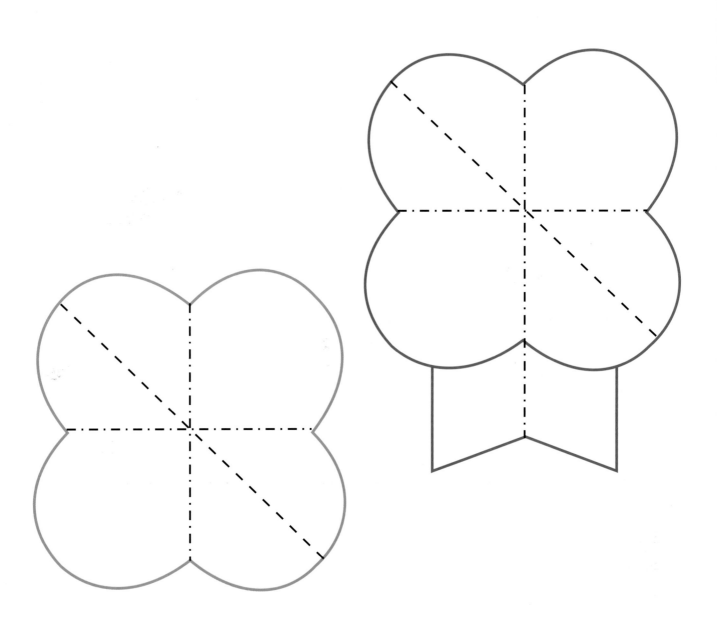

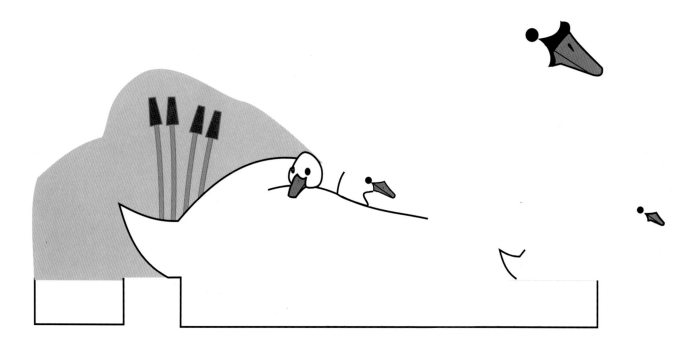

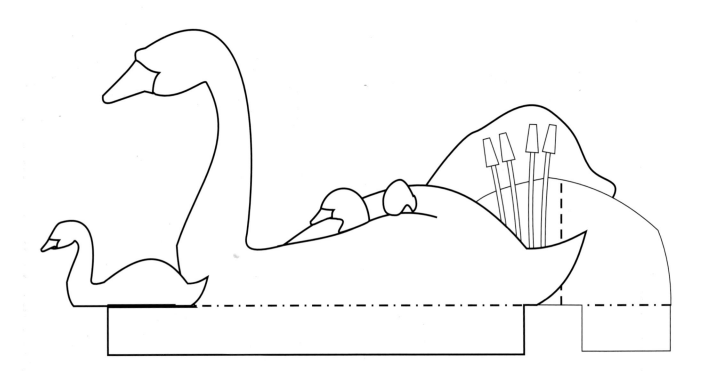

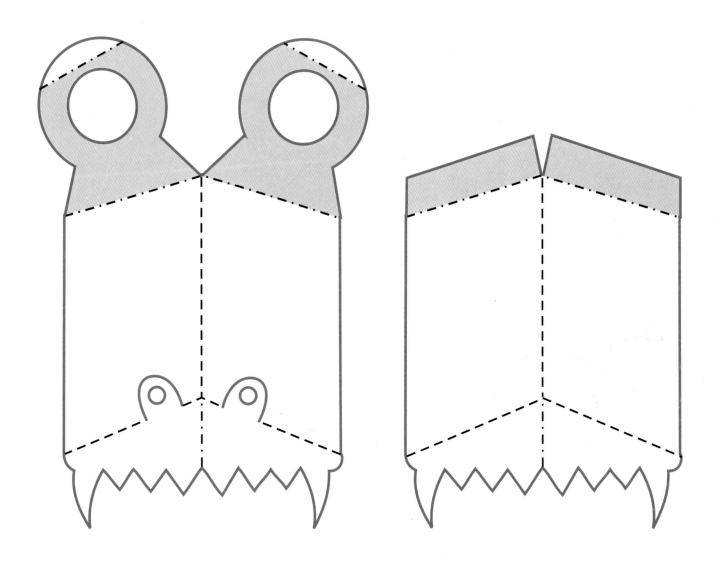

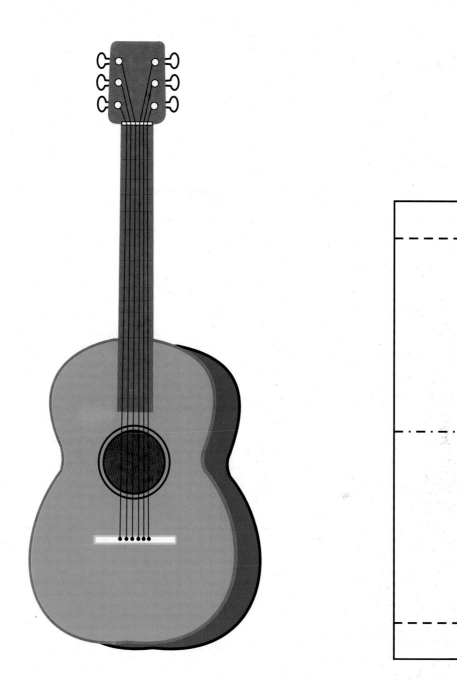

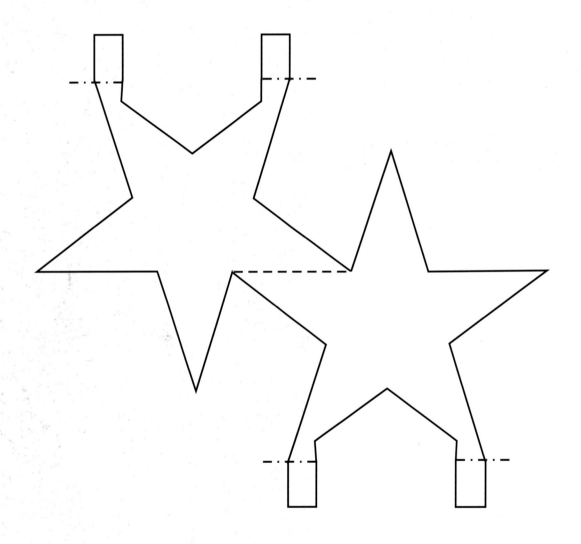

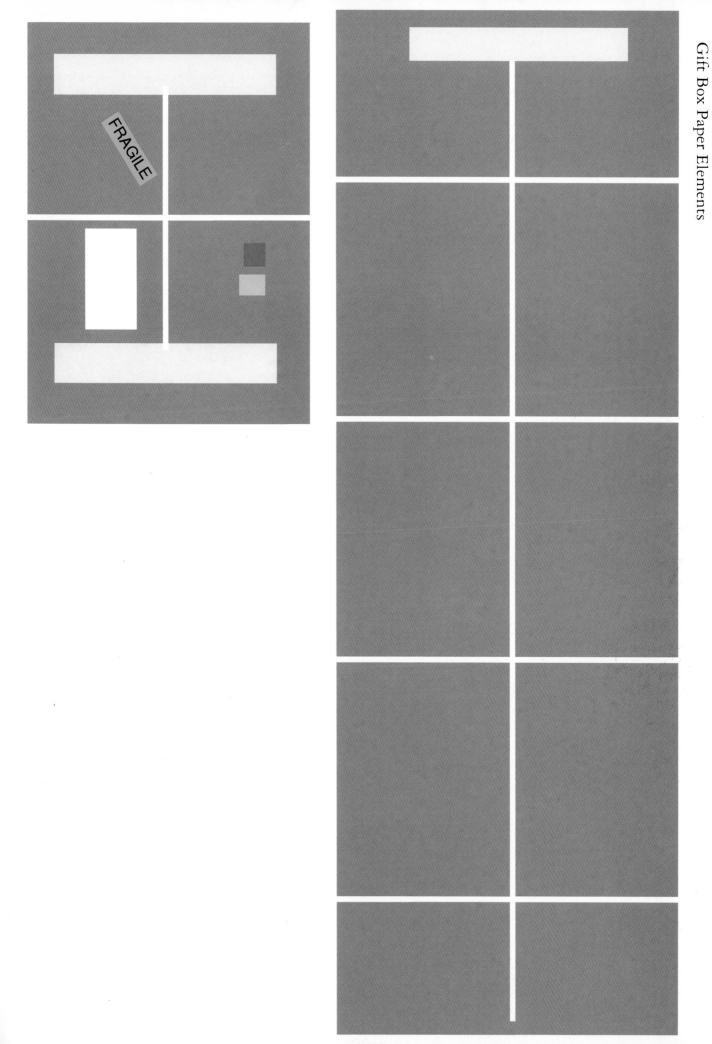

FRAGILE

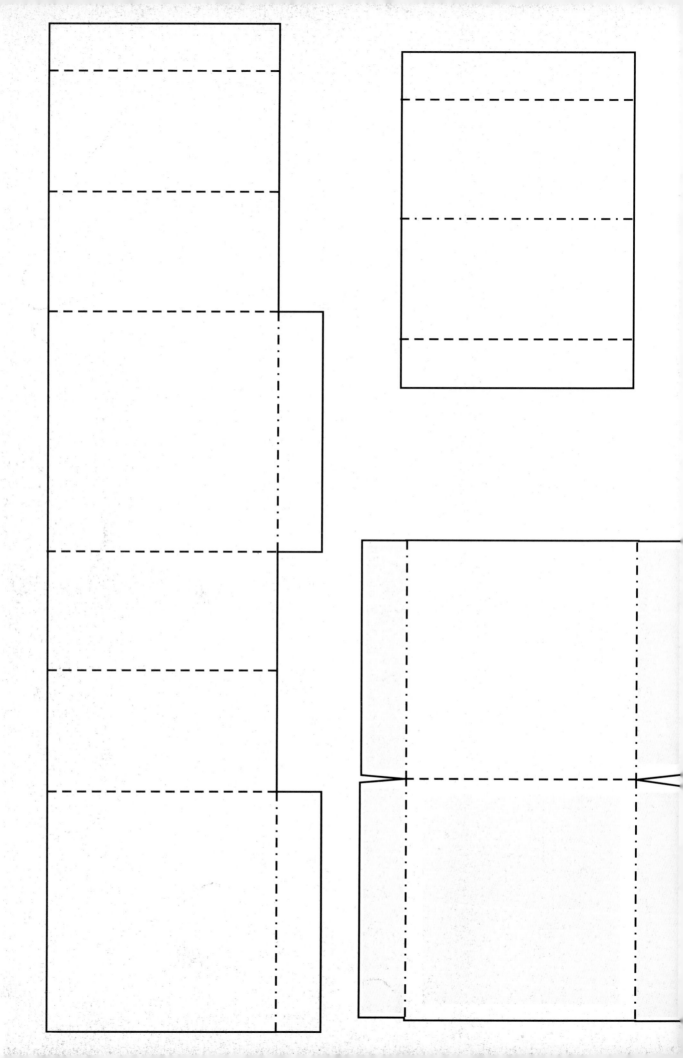

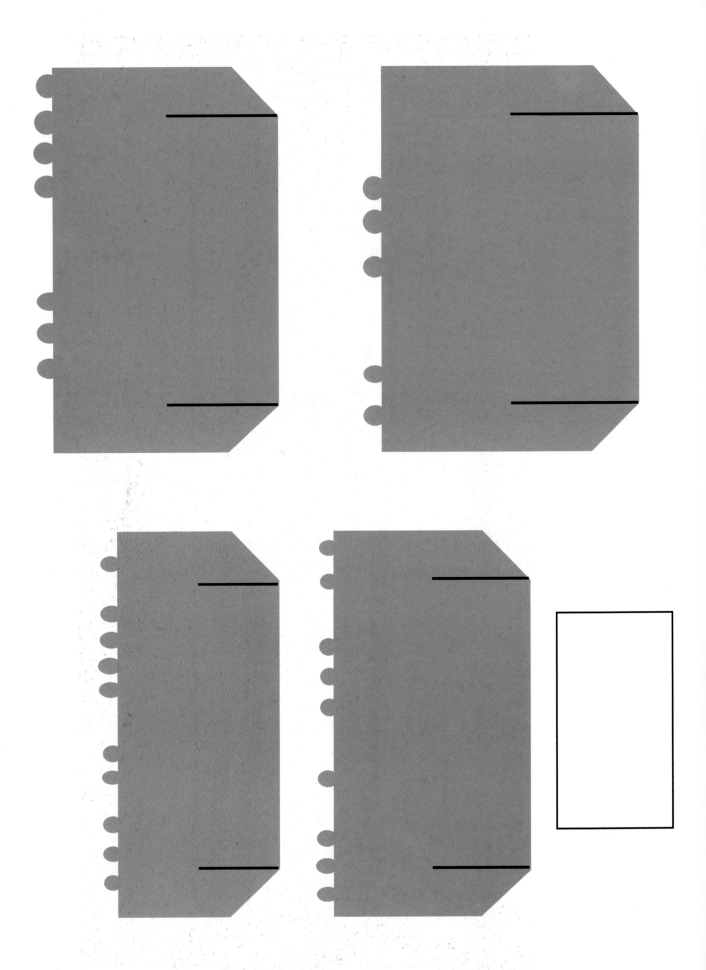

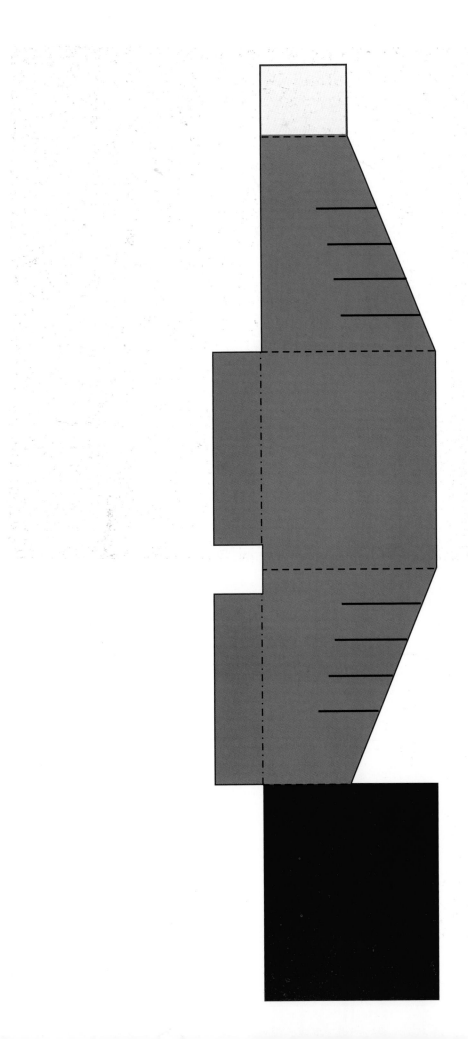

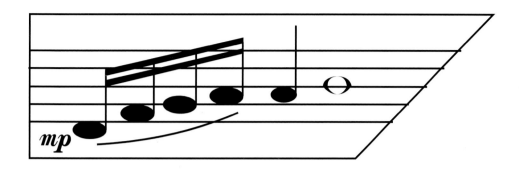

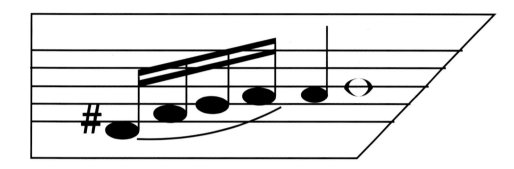

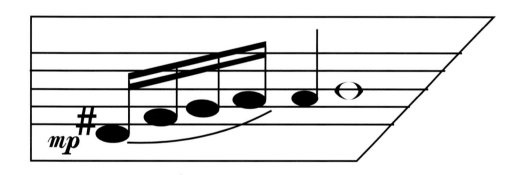

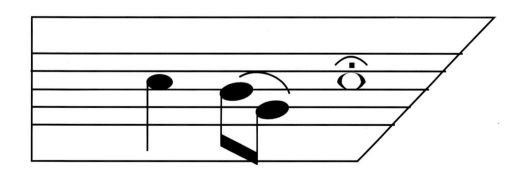

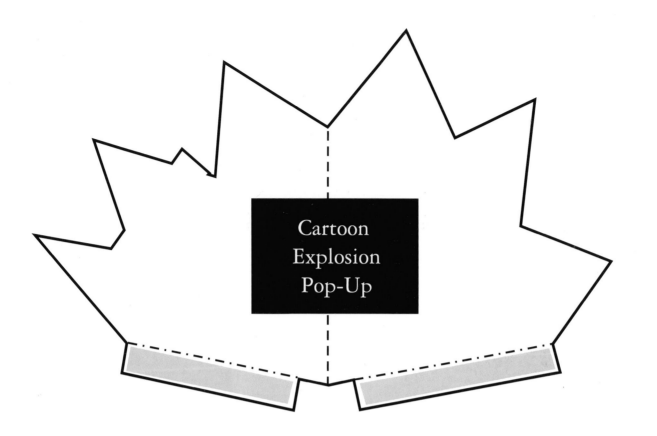

Cartoon
Explosion
Pop-Up

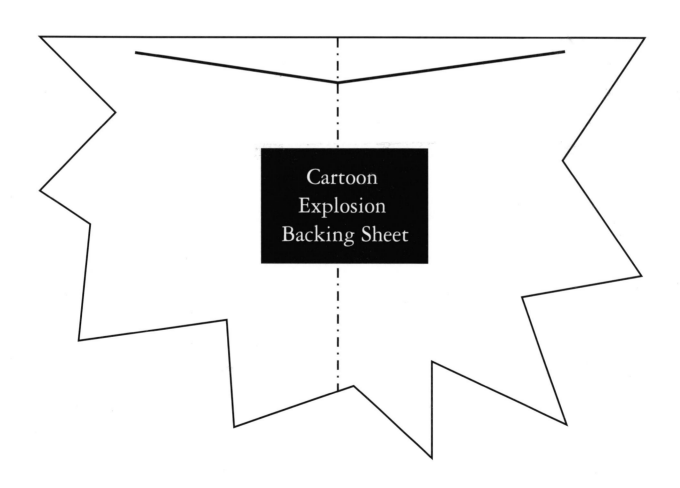

Cartoon
Explosion
Backing Sheet

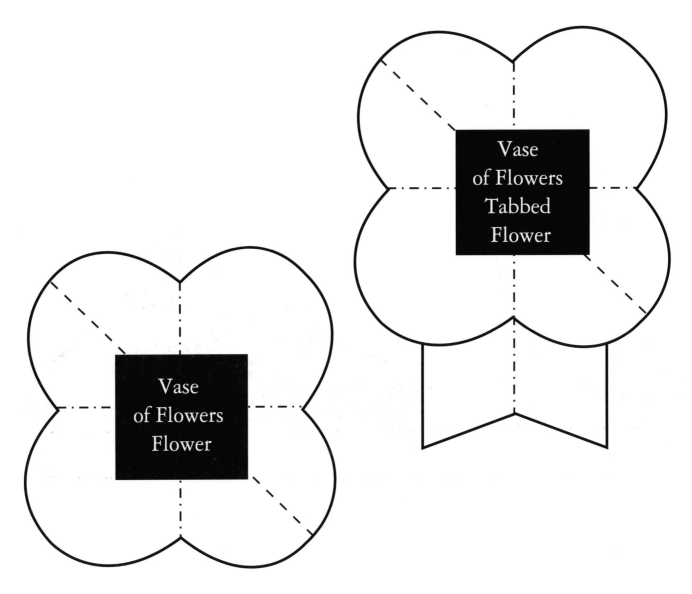

Vase
of Flowers
Tabbed
Flower

Vase
of Flowers
Flower

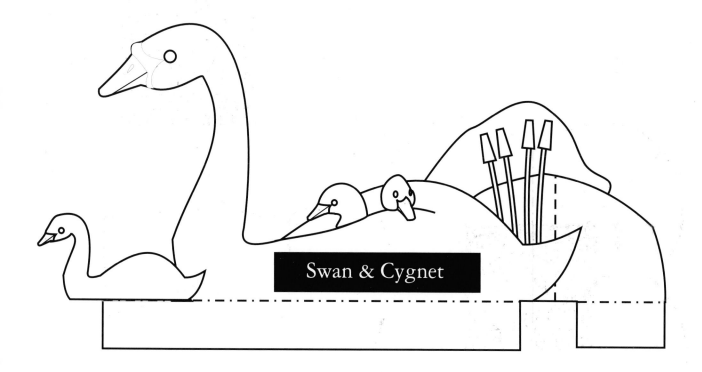

Swan & Cygnet

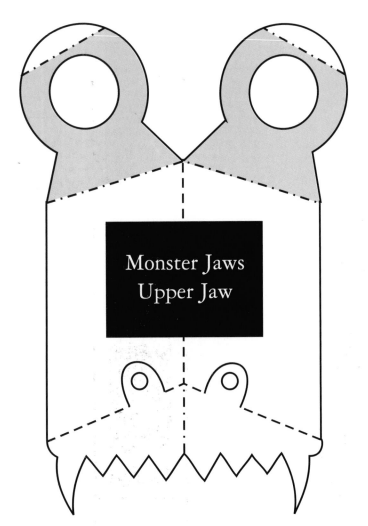

Monster Jaws
Upper Jaw

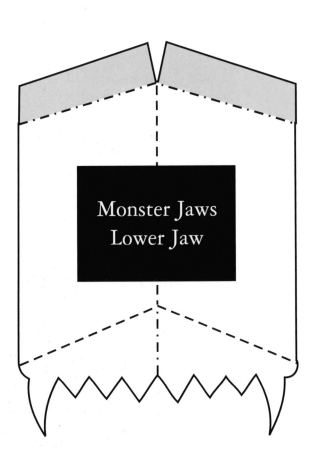

Monster Jaws
Lower Jaw

Guitar

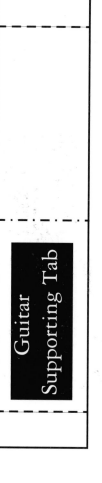

Guitar
Supporting Tab

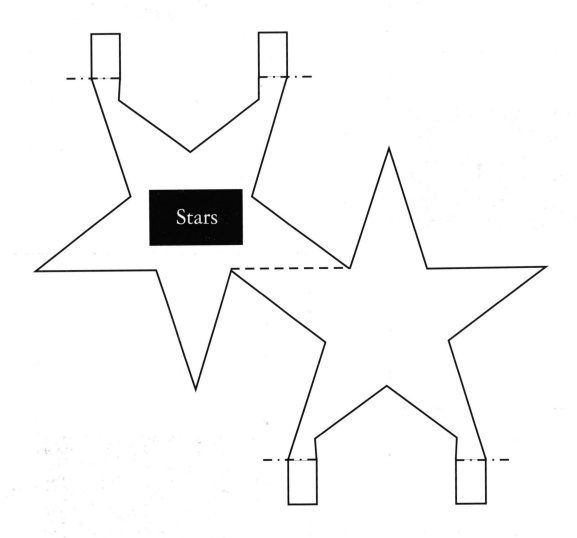

Stars

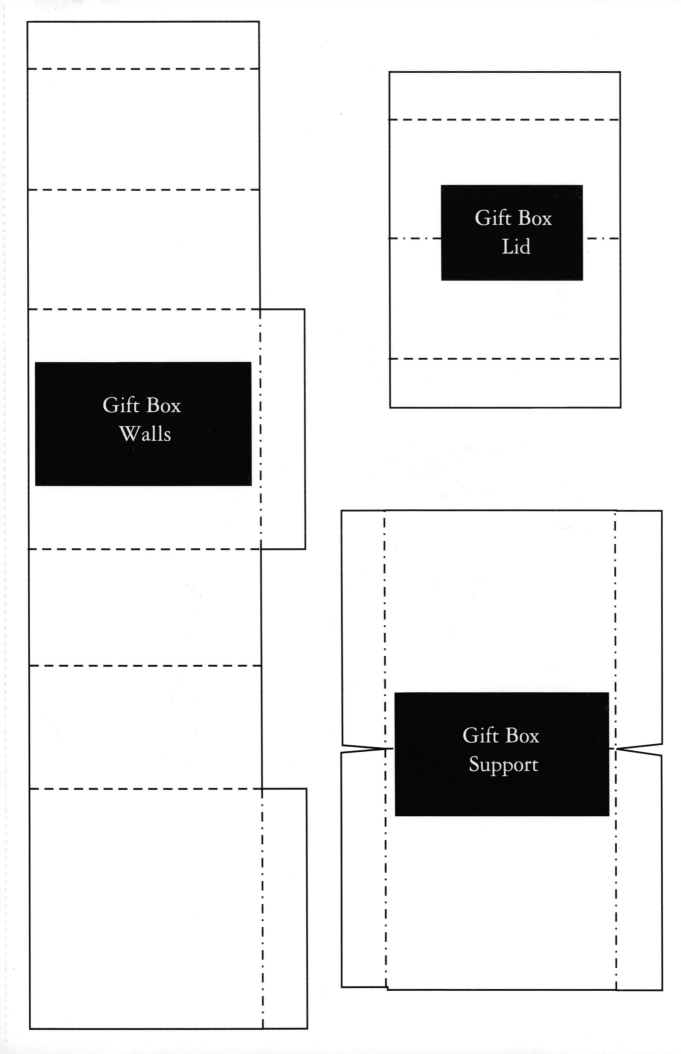

Gift Box
Lid

Gift Box
Walls

Gift Box
Support

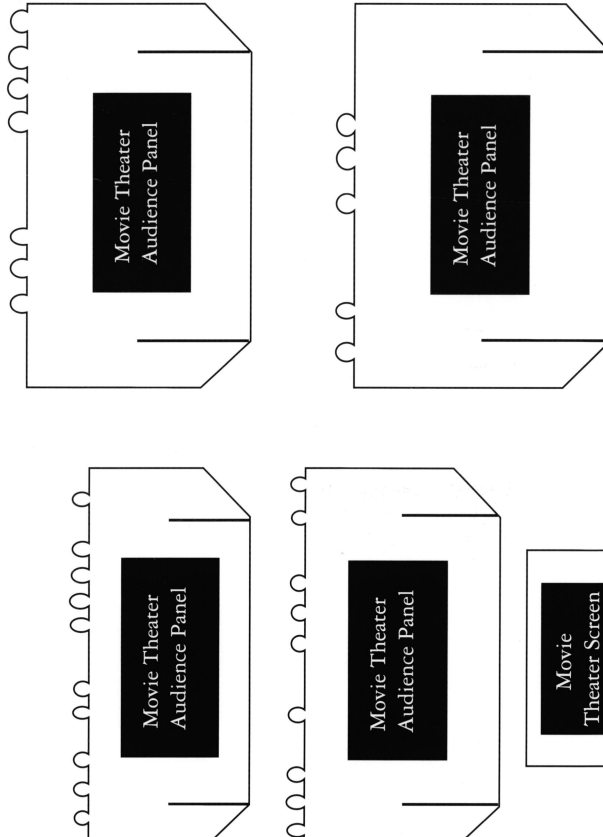

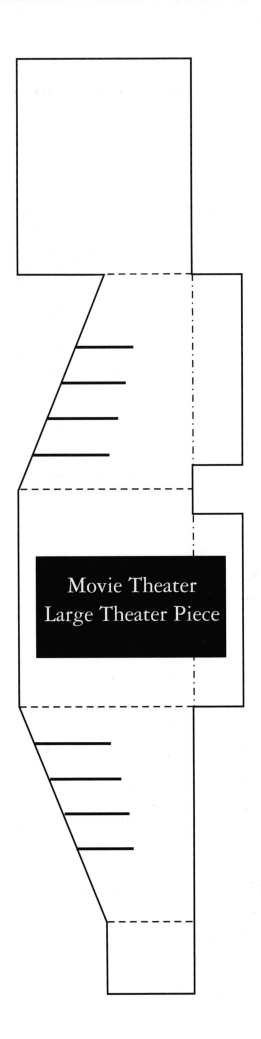

Movie Theater
Large Theater Piece

Note: To make an accurate
template, enlarge on a
photocopier at 125%.

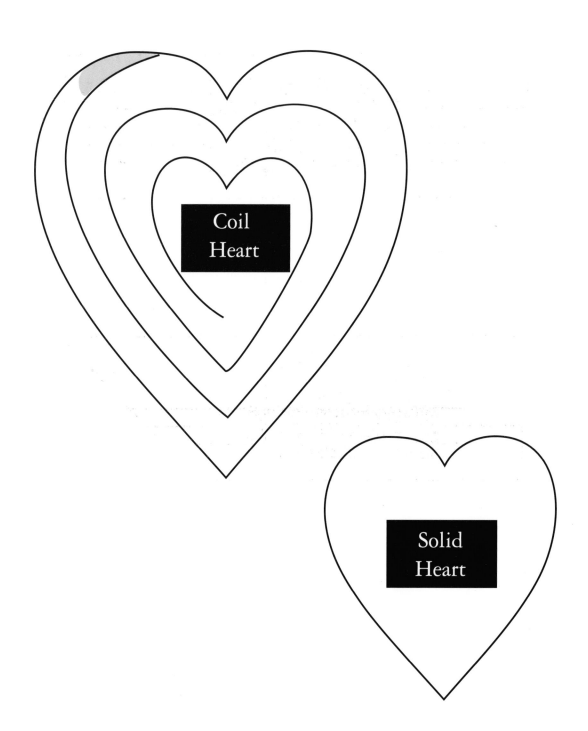

Coil
Heart

Solid
Heart

Musical Score
Rectangular Shape

Musical Score
Beveled Shape

Celebration
Wine Bottle

VIN

Wine Glass

Celebration Large Strap

Celebration Small Strap